D0856823

J. Robert Oppenheimer

Theoretical Physicist, Atomic Pioneer

Toney Allman

BLACKBIRCH PRESS

An imprint of Thomson Gale, a part of The Thomson Corporation

THOMSON

GALE

Detroit • New York • San Francisco • San Diego • New Haven, Conn.
Waterville, Maine • London • Munich

Photo Credits: cover, pages 23, 50 © Time-Life Pictures/Getty Images; page 15 AIP Neils Bohr Library/Margrathe Bohr Collection; page 17 © Bettmann/CORBIS; pages 10, 27, 29, 33, 35, 39, 41, 45, 47, 48, 54 © CORBIS; pages 13, 25 Corel Corporation; page 6 © Getty Images; pages 5, 18, 26, 37, 42, 43 Los Alamos National Laboratory; page 59 © Richard T. Nowitz/CORBIS; page 7 © Oppenheimer Archives/CORBIS; page 14 © Royalty-Free/CORBIS; page 49 © Smithsonian Institution; pages 22, 31 Steve Zmina

LIBRARY OF CONGRESS CATALOGING-IN-PUBLICATION DATA

Allman, Toney.
  J. Robert Oppenheimer / by Toney Allman.
    p. cm. — (Giants of science)
  Includes bibliographical references and index.
  ISBN 1-56711-889-5 (hardcover : alk. paper)
  1. Oppenheimer, J. Robert, 1904–1967—Juvenile literature. 2. Atomic bomb—United States—History—Juvenile literature. 3. Physicists—United States—Biography—Juvenile literature. I. Title. II. Series.
  QC16.O62A54 2005
  530'.092—dc22
                                                                    2004011199

CONTENTS

The Trinity Test

The time was zero minus twenty minutes. It was not yet sunrise at the Trinity test-bombing range in the Alamogordo, New Mexico, desert, on July 16, 1945. Dr. J. Robert Oppenheimer stood in the control bunker staring toward the test tower, five miles away, where the "gadget" waited. He was tense and anxious, afraid that the test would fail. Other scientists and military men waited with him, here and at other observation posts, but Oppenheimer felt alone. He was pale and unshaven. His eyes were tired. He gripped a post with white knuckles and spoke to no one. He was a theoretical physicist, a scientist dedicated to understanding the way the universe is built. Yet he was now the scientific head of a project in which the successful outcome of this test was his overwhelming responsibility.

> "We felt the world would never be the same again."
>
> J. ROBERT OPPENHEIMER

At zero minus three seconds, Oppenheimer pressed his hands tightly over his eyes. He barely breathed. Then, the time was zero. Suddenly, in absolute silence, a huge white flash lit up the New Mexico desert. It was brighter than the sun at noon, brighter than anyone had ever imagined light could be.

A giant fireball rose into the sky from the place the gadget had been. It was brilliant with glowing colors of gold, green, orange, red, and purple. They were the colors of radioactivity boiling in the fireball. A wave of heat and a shock of sound traveled across the desert. The shock wave knocked some of the watching scientists and military people off their feet. Thunder roared, boomed, and echoed as a tremendous column of smoke spiraled out of the fireball. It towered higher than the highest mountain on Earth and then formed a giant mushroom-shaped cloud.

The first atomic bomb had worked. The observers reacted with relief and awe at the stupendous thing humans had created. They all knew that they had witnessed the dawn of a new age. Some people stood in stunned silence. Some laughed. Some cried. J. Robert Oppenheimer gazed at the results of the creation he had worked so hard and so long to bring about and remembered a line from Hindu scripture: "Now I am become Death, the destroyer of worlds."[1]

"The War Is Over"

For the preceding twenty-eight months, Oppenheimer had directed the work at the Los Alamos, New Mexico, laboratory assigned to the task of building the atomic bomb. By 1945, thousands of people were working for and with him in the largest scientific project ever attempted by the United States.

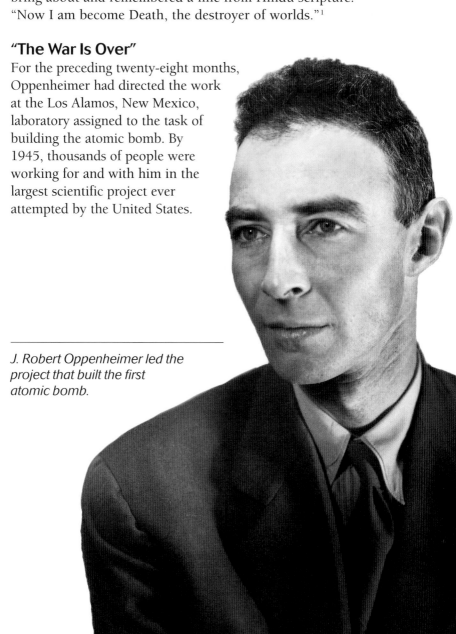

J. Robert Oppenheimer led the project that built the first atomic bomb.

This photograph, taken on July 16, 1945, at the Trinity testing range in New Mexico, shows the world's first atomic bomb blast.

The country and the world were at war. "The war is over,"[2] exulted one general in response to the successful Trinity test. There was elation among all the watching scientists and military people that, with this new weapon, they now had the means to win the war. There was also appalled shock and dismay over the awful destructive power they had unleashed.

By 1945, World War II had been going on for years. The Nazis in Germany and the militarists in Japan had wanted to conquer the world. The Allies, including the United States, had lived through agonizing years of battles, fear, and suffering. Millions had died. Finally, Germany had been defeated in May, but Japan fought on. It was predicted that a million more lives would be lost in a land invasion to finally defeat Japan. All during the war years, the United States had been conducting a secret project known as the Manhattan Project. With plants, factories, and laboratories hidden throughout America, the Manhattan Project was a unified national effort to invent an atom bomb and end the war.

The Atomic Age Begins

At Los Alamos, Oppenheimer led the difficult and sometimes desperate efforts of the scientists to actually build the bomb that no one was sure could be built at all. At Trinity, in the

Alamogordo desert, they proved they had done it. The atomic age was born. The atom bomb was used on Japan and accomplished its purpose with horrible efficiency. Japan surrendered, the war ended, the secret project was revealed, and J. Robert Oppenheimer became an unlikely American hero. The gentle physicist with the sad eyes became known to the world as "The Father of the Atomic Bomb."

Privileged Beginnings

J. Robert Oppenheimer was born in New York City on April 22, 1904. His father, Julius Oppenheimer, had come to New York as an immigrant from Germany when he was just seventeen years old. With the help of an uncle, he became a prosperous businessman and fabric merchant and was so successful that he eventually became president of his company. His wife, Ella, was an artist and art teacher before she married.

Young Robert was born into a wealthy, artistic, and intellectual home. The furnishings of the family's Riverside Drive apartment were in beautiful taste. Great artwork hung upon the walls. The household was quiet and dignified. Both parents were Jewish, but not religious. Education, gentility, good manners, and moral behavior were the values they meant to pass on to their children.

The wealthy Julius and Ella Oppenheimer gave their son Robert a protected and privileged life.

Julius and Ella were determined to give every advantage to their firstborn child. At first, they planned to name their new son Robert, but Julius decided that was not distinguished enough. He thought a longer name would be more impressive, so using his first initial, he named his son J. Robert Oppenheimer. The J. did not stand for anything at all.

The Good Little Boy

Robert was cherished by both his parents. He was a thin and sickly child whose mother carefully nursed him through illnesses that included tubercular fever, flu, and polio. The family revolved around him. He was coddled and protected, so much so that he did not have a normal childhood. He was not allowed to play in the streets or parks with other boys. The family had maids, a butler, and a chauffeur who drove Robert wherever he went. He was carefully taught not to make noise, to always be polite, and to speak intelligently with adults. By the time he was five, Robert played quietly by himself or read books. His powerful intelligence was already obvious, and his father saw to it that he received all the books he could want. He was a very well-behaved boy who never caused trouble, but he had no friends, played no sports or games, and had no idea how to get along with children his own age.

When Robert was five, the family took a trip to Europe. In Germany, he met his grandfather and other members of his extended family. Robert's cousins thought he was very strange. He sat in the house and read a book while they played noisily outside. One day, Robert's grandfather took him for a walk in the country and gave him some interesting rocks as a gift. Robert was fascinated. He wanted to know all about each kind of rock, how it was made, and why each one was different from the other. It was his first scientific interest.

Back in America, Robert began a rock collection that grew rapidly. His bedroom was loaded with rocks, and he acquired many rock collecting books. By the time he was eleven, he joined the New York Mineralogical Club. All the other members were adults. When he was twelve, he gave a talk on rock collecting at a club meeting. The club members were shocked at the extent of his knowledge.

School Days

Robert was sent to a private school in New York City to which he was driven each morning by the chauffeur. To the teachers, he was the star pupil. To the other students, he was an awkward, unpopular boy who did not fit in. He was teased because he could not even catch a ball. He was laughed at for his grown-up ways. Robert wanted to be liked and even to be popular, but he did not know how. Already, he was so much smarter than the other boys that his interests were very different from theirs. When he was nine, he could speak both Latin and Greek and was proud of the ability. He was so gifted and quick-thinking that he could not understand that others could only slowly grasp concepts that were simple for him. Other boys just thought he was stuck-up and strange.

Finally, the school principal talked to Robert's parents about teaching him something other than academics. Robert was so inactive that he even refused to walk up the stairs at school. He always insisted on waiting for the elevator. Dutifully, Julius and Ella enrolled Robert in tennis lessons. He was inept, clumsy, and very uninterested in the sport. Next, his parents sent him to a summer camp. Robert tried his best and stuck it out, but the experience was a miserable one for him. The other boys taunted and harassed him the whole summer. Their cruel nickname for him was "Cutie." In academics and in intellectual activities, Robert excelled, but he did not know how to make friends.

Growing Up

When Robert was eight, his brother Frank was born. Despite the difference in their ages, Robert and Frank became good friends. Frank looked up to his older brother, and Robert enjoyed taking care of Frank. By the time he was in high school, Robert at last had two friends his own age. These classmates were intellectually gifted also, and the boys were

Despite their eight-year age difference, Robert (right) and his younger brother Frank remained close throughout their lives.

able to talk about common interests such as science, art, or new Broadway plays.

When Robert was sixteen, he finally found something athletic that he could do. His father bought him a sailboat to use at their Long Island summer home, and Robert took great joy in it. He became a skilled sailor and took his friends and little Frank out sailing, in both good weather and bad. When the waves were calm, he often spent the day on the water reading. When the waves were high or storms were brewing, he used all his skill to provide an exciting ride. He discovered the fun of recklessness and risks. His parents were upset with him for exposing himself, his brother, and his friends to danger. He loved to take them out sailing in the middle of thunderstorms. The teenager ignored his parents' concerns. He was adventurous, bookish, and rebellious, all at the same time.

Despite his growing rebellion, Robert continued to absorb all that he could learn at school. In his senior year, he took all the science and math courses available plus French and German. With ten courses that last year, he had ten As. He was a phenomenal learner and interested in everything from chemistry to poetry. He graduated from high school in 1921 and was accepted at Harvard for the following fall.

Interlude

The summer before college, Robert's parents took him to Europe for a pleasure trip. On the trip, he became very ill with dysentery, which left him with colitis and other digestive problems. He came home too weak and sick to go to college that year. It was an unhappy time for him. He stayed home in his parents' apartment, where he read and wrote melancholy poetry. His mother prepared a special diet for him, but he would not follow it. He was rude to his parents and their friends, refused to socialize with them, and locked himself in his room and brooded. His signs of depression became so bad that his father felt something must be done. He went to one of Robert's favorite high school teachers, Herbert Smith, and asked him to accompany Robert out West for a trip of healing and strengthening. Robert was furious. He did not want a nursemaid and refused to go. His father insisted, however, and off to New Mexico went Smith with Robert in tow.

"When I was ten or twelve years old, minerals, writing poems and reading, and building with blocks still—architecture—were the three themes that I did, not because they were something I had companionship in or because they had any relation to school, but just for the hell of it."

J. ROBERT OPPENHEIMER

All through that spring and summer, the two companions hiked, rode horses, camped out, and visited ranches. It turned out to be an exciting, joyful experience for Robert.

He discovered a surprising skill at handling horses. He adored the West with its mountains, deserts, and wilderness areas. Smith discovered that despite Robert's weak, frail body, the boy had determination and bravery. The trip was a great success. Robert came home to New York in the fall tanned, muscular, still very slim, but healthy in body and spirit. He had turned into a handsome young man, six feet tall and ready for independence.

Harvard

Robert went off to Harvard in the autumn of 1922. From the beginning, he delighted in college life. He loved being free of his parents and their protectiveness. He ate whatever he wanted, whenever he wanted, and practically lived on chocolate and peanut butter. He was thrilled with all the classes available to him and enchanted by the huge library where he spent hours every day. At first, his main academic interest was chemistry, but he discovered the new field of physics and turned to it along with mathematics as the way to understand the universe.

He had a huge intellectual energy and took extra classes every semester. He made friends, too, who liked him but often had trouble understanding him. Although he was brilliant in class, he was emotionally immature in many ways. He could be arrogant about his knowledge. His classmates and

Before college, Oppenheimer spent time in New Mexico. Robert fell in love with the West and soon learned to handle horses.

professors thought he asked too many questions, and he remained impatient with those who could not learn as quickly as he could. Still, he was likeable, charming, and full of fun. He could be warm and generous and was embarrassed and remorseful when he realized he had hurt a friend's feelings.

Every summer, during vacations, he took friends along with him back to New Mexico, to the wilderness he had grown to love. During one of these trips, he and a friend were camping overnight and ran out of food. His friend offered him a cigarette to fight off hunger pangs. Robert became addicted to tobacco and continued to smoke regularly when he returned to school.

Experimental Physics in England

In 1925, Robert graduated from Harvard summa cum laude (with highest distinction) after just three years of study. At that time, physics was a rapidly advancing science and a new way to understand the universe. There were very few experts, almost all of them in Europe. Robert wanted to have a part in the discoveries. The physicists were beginning to unlock the secrets of the atom.

All matter, whether living or nonliving, whether solid, liquid, or gas, is made up of tiny particles called atoms. They are the building blocks of the universe. Atoms, in turn, are composed of even tinier parts called subatomic particles. The electron is one subatomic particle. Electrons have a negative electrical charge and orbit around a nucleus at the center of the atom. In the nucleus are the positively charged protons, also subatomic particles. The negative and positive electrical charges of the electrons and protons attract each other and hold the atom together. Different kinds of matter have different numbers of electrons and protons in their atoms. This is what makes helium helium, for instance, and not uranium. An atom of helium has two protons and two electrons while a uranium atom has ninety-two protons and ninety-two electrons.

By 1925, physicists knew that most atomic nuclei are stable, which means that they hold together very tightly. Other

An atomic model shows electrons orbiting a nucleus. In this illustration, the nucleus is shown as a solid, but it really consists of subatomic particles.

electron

orbital path

nucleus

atomic nuclei, such as uranium nuclei, are unstable because they do not hold together tightly and, instead, emit radioactive rays. This radioactivity is a form of decay that is produced as small parts of the atom's nucleus break off naturally.

Even though atoms and subatomic particles could not be seen, their behavior could be studied using the radioactivity from unstable atoms. Physicists had built experimental machines in which they could shoot radioactive particles at other atoms and knock out the nuclei. They also learned how to shoot a stream of electrons at stable and unstable matter and studied the way electrons moved through the different kinds of matter. They were learning how the atoms of the different kinds of matter were built, how the atoms behaved, and how much energy held atoms together.

Ernest Rutherford, the physicist who had discovered the atomic nucleus and protons, was the director of the Cavendish Laboratory at Cambridge University in England, where most of the experiments with atoms and electrons were taking place. Working with him was Joseph Thomson, who had isolated the electron and measured its size. Niels Bohr, who had used mathematics to map the orbits that electrons made in different kinds of matter and discovered that radioactivity came from the nucleus, often visited Cavendish. Robert Oppenheimer was accepted as a graduate student at Cambridge and went to the Cavendish Laboratory to learn from these great scientists.

He was not very good at experimental physics. Thomson assigned Oppenheimer the task of preparing thin metal films for use in experiments on how electrons penetrate matter. He performed the work badly, could not achieve correct results, and had no patience for delicate experimental tasks. He was so upset with his failure to do experiments well that a friend found him lying on the floor of his room one day rolling back and forth and moaning. He was still troubled by depression when his academic life was not going well, and he was not used to failure.

Along with performing experiments in physics, Oppenheimer also began to study theoretical physics, especially quantum theory, the new and revolutionary way to understand the behavior of energy and subatomic particles. Quantum theory explains mathematically that an electron sometimes acts like a particle and sometimes as a wave. Energy in streams of subatomic particles also acts like a wave sometimes and a particle at other times. These energy units are called quanta. With quantum theory, physicists could explore mathematically the behavior of subatomic particles. The theory helped them to understand the way energy moved from one point to another. Oppenheimer developed some mathematical ways to explain atomic energy waves and had two

Oppenheimer learned from eminent scientists such as Niels Bohr (pictured) while a student at England's Cavendish Laboratory.

papers about quantum theory published while he was still a student at Cambridge. It was in the theory of why things happened that he excelled, not in the experiments about how things happened.

Studying Theoretical Physics

Oppenheimer left Cambridge in 1926 and went to Germany, to the University of Göttingen, where the best theoretical physicists were studying quantum theory. He studied under and with James Franck, Max Born, Paul Dirac, and Ed Condon, all powerful theorists. Professors and students were learning together. Quantum theory and theoretical physics were so new that anyone who understood the ideas could make a contribution. Oppenheimer was quickly recognized as a brilliant mind in the new, exciting field. At last, Oppenheimer's habit of posing questions was appreciated. His mathematical questions and ideas helped extend quantum theory and added to the knowledge in the field. Together, he and Born worked out how quantum theory applied to different kinds of matter and published their results.

Germany was not all physics for Oppenheimer. He continued to be intellectually interested in everything. He learned Italian so that he could read the poet Dante and joined a literary group. He immersed himself in philosophy, music, and poetry in his spare time. His friend Dirac could not understand why he wasted his time with such impractical things, but Oppenheimer persisted. All learning was worthwhile to him. Oppenheimer got a new name while he was in Germany, too. His friends and teachers began to call him "Oppie." He was still arrogant and a snob about academics, but he had become a lovable friend and an admired colleague.

In 1927, Oppenheimer received his

> "The kind of person that I admire most would be one who becomes extraordinarily good at doing a lot of things but still maintains a tear-stained countenance."
>
> J. ROBERT OPPENHEIMER

After receiving his doctorate in physics, Oppenheimer moved from Germany to Switzerland to study under Wolfgang Pauli (pictured).

doctorate "with distinction" from Göttingen. He was homesick for America and yearned to create an advanced school of theoretical physics in the United States, but first he needed to expand his knowledge of mathematics and quantum theory. With a postdoctoral fellowship, he went to Zurich, Switzerland, to work under Wolfgang Pauli, who had discovered that

Oppenheimer overcame his carelessness in mathematical calculations and established himself as an extraordinary thinker.

electrons spin within their orbits. Pauli thought Oppenheimer was brilliant. He was quick with new ideas and able to get to the heart of mathematical problems with ease. Pauli worried, though, over how sloppy Oppenheimer was with his mathematical calculations. "His ideas are always very interesting but his calculations are always wrong,"[3] Pauli once said about

Oppenheimer. A fellow student noticed, however, that while the calculations had errors, Oppenheimer's conclusions were usually correct. Pauli helped Oppenheimer to discipline his impatience and stop speeding over the mathematical details. By the time he finally sailed for the United States, Oppenheimer had established a reputation among physicists as a phenomenal thinker.

California Professor

Once he returned home, Oppenheimer received offers of teaching positions from several universities. In 1929, at the age of twenty-six, he accepted two positions and agreed to teach half the year at the University of California at Berkeley and half the year at the California Institute of Technology. He taught theoretical physics and quantum theory to graduate students and pursued his own research as well.

As a professor, Oppenheimer was not immediately successful. In rapid, mumbling speech, he threw so many new ideas at his confused students that they were completely lost. Several went to the head of the physics department to complain that Oppenheimer went too fast, and the material was too difficult. They were encouraged to stick out the course, but soon Oppenheimer paid a visit to the department head, too. He complained that he was unable to present enough material; the course went too slowly and his students were not progressing.

Over a period of several months, Oppenheimer learned to slow down, and as the students began to understand the exciting new material, they became very attached to their chain-smoking professor. During class, he smoked furiously with one hand and scribbled formulas on the blackboard with the other. The students watched, hypnotized, as they waited for the day he would try to write with the cigarette and smoke the chalk. To the disappointment of some, he never made that mistake.

As time passed, Oppenheimer turned into an eloquent and charismatic teacher and attracted more and more gifted students. His groups of students became so enthralled with him that they followed him as he moved back and forth between

Cal Tech and Berkeley. Eventually, he turned Berkeley into the best center for theoretical physics in America.

Oppenheimer's reputation as a researcher grew, also. His tools were not the big machines and laboratory equipment of the experimental physicists. Oppenheimer's research tools were a piece of chalk, a blackboard, and his questioning mind. Sometimes, a whole day would pass while he stared, lost in thought, at a blackboard full of his mathematical formulas. During his time as a professor, he published several papers in quantum theory and was recognized by his colleagues as a genius theoretical physicist.

Experimental physicist Ernest Lawrence was another gifted young professor at Berkeley. He and Oppenheimer became good friends, and Oppenheimer helped Lawrence with his most important experiment. Lawrence was trying to build a cyclotron, a particle accelerator. It would use electricity and big magnets to speed up a subatomic particle stream so that Lawrence could study atomic nuclei. Whenever Lawrence ran into trouble in building his complex machine, he came to Oppenheimer for help with the theory. Oppenheimer was so much help in solving these problems that Lawrence proudly began to call him "my theoretical physicist."[4]

> "The reason Oppenheimer knows so much is that it's easy when you learn ten times as fast as other physicists and remember everything."
>
> RAYMOND BIRGE,
> BERKELEY PHYSICS DEPARTMENT HEAD

Physics Advances

While Oppenheimer and Lawrence were teaching and doing atomic research in California, a physicist in England, James Chadwick, made a critical discovery. In 1932, he demonstrated that an atom's nucleus did not consist solely of protons. Chadwick discovered neutrons, subatomic particles in the nucleus that had no electrical charge. Neutrons were a significant discovery, because they are large in size and weight compared to other subatomic particles and because they lack a charge.

It had always been difficult to study the atomic nucleus with particle streams of negatively charged electrons. The electrons' charges meant that they were often repelled or sucked in by the charges of the electrons or nuclei that scientists tried to examine. Neutrons, however, presented no such problem. Since they had no charge, they could be shot easily through the electrons' orbits, directly toward the atom's nucleus. Also, neutrons are massive compared to the tiny electron. A particle stream of massive, chargeless neutrons shot at different atomic nuclei had a good chance of hitting the nuclei.

All over the world, experimental physicists took advantage of the discovery of the neutron and used neutron particle streams to study atomic nuclei. Then, in 1939, a momentous event occurred. Neutrons shot at uranium atoms actually split the unstable nuclei in two. This splitting was named fission.

Nuclear fission meant the discovery of a new and powerful force, nuclear energy. Whenever a nucleus is split, a part of its binding force is released as enormous energy. If this new force could be harnessed and controlled, it could be remarkably valuable. Theoretically, with enough fissioning atoms, huge amounts of nuclear energy could be made available to humanity as heat for power or as an explosive weapon.

Fascism, Fission, and War

Tremendous excitement spread throughout the physics world, but this excitement was tinged with dread. The splitting of the atom happened in Italy and Germany at the same time that World War II was beginning. The Nazi Party in Germany, its Fascist allies in Italy, and the militarists in Japan had begun their war of aggression. They aimed to establish dictatorships over the peoples of the world. These Axis powers believed in the superiority of their races over all other races. In Europe, Jews especially were attacked and persecuted as the Nazis took over. Theoretical physics told the scientists that fission could be used not just for energy but also for weapons of unimaginable destruction. The dread was that

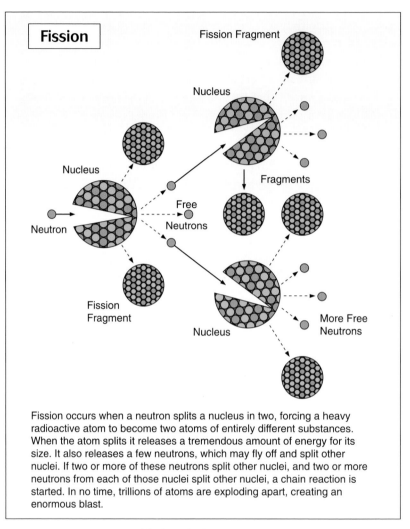

Fission

Fission Fragment

Nucleus

Nucleus

Neutron

Free
Neutrons

Fragments

Fission
Fragment

Nucleus

More Free
Neutrons

Fission occurs when a neutron splits a nucleus in two, forcing a heavy radioactive atom to become two atoms of entirely different substances. When the atom splits it releases a tremendous amount of energy for its size. It also releases a few neutrons, which may fly off and split other nuclei. If two or more of these neutrons split other nuclei, and two or more neutrons from each of those nuclei split other nuclei, a chain reaction is started. In no time, trillions of atoms are exploding apart, creating an enormous blast.

Nazi scientists could already be at work on such a weapon.

Many of the physicists in Europe were Jewish or had Jewish relatives. They fled from the Nazis to America and talked to their colleagues about the possible use of nuclear energy in weapons. They encouraged other physicists to research the new force and to maintain careful secrecy about any success.

Albert Einstein, himself a refugee and the most famous scientist of the century, urged President Franklin Roosevelt to help and encourage research into the feasibility of a fission bomb. Roosevelt agreed and granted a small amount of money to several university laboratories to aid them in their research. The scientists' work was coordinated and named the Uranium Committee. Oppenheimer's good friend Ernest Lawrence was one of the physicists in the project.

Along with other American scientists, Oppenheimer immediately recognized the possibilities in nuclear fission. He lectured to his students about how nuclear energy from fission might be used to produce a bomb. Dynamite, or TNT, explodes just because its energy release burns hot enough and fast enough to be an explosion instead of heat or a fire. In the same way, the energy released during fission also could be turned into an explosion. The binding force of nuclear energy is so much more powerful than the energy in TNT that the resulting explosion could be incredibly great. Theoretically, all it would take would be to fission enough atoms fast enough— trillions of atoms in millionths of a second.

For Oppenheimer, a fission bomb was an interesting intellectual exercise, but it did not seem to be of any immediate

Albert Einstein (left) encouraged American scientists like Oppenheimer to research the possibility of a fission bomb.

practical value. Science's ability to create such a nuclear reaction seemed decades away. Besides, Oppenheimer was not really interested in weapons. He was involved in a mathematical study of cosmic rays from stars and space. With quantum theory, he mathematically described the existence of black holes and neutron stars, but was so far ahead of science's discovery of these phenomena that he was ignored.

World War II

Oppenheimer's thoughts remained in the stars, but his heart turned with outrage to the Nazi menace. He had Jewish relatives in Germany. He and his brother Frank, who had also become a physicist, arranged to rescue their family from Germany and take care of them in America. Frank and Robert were still very close, and both had become absorbed in world political affairs. In response to the injustices and oppression around the world, Frank joined the American Communist Party. Robert was attracted to some of the ideas and sympathized with his brother, but he heard too much about Communist injustices to trust the Communist Party. Still, many of his friends had Communist interests.

In 1939, Oppenheimer met Kitty Harrison. She was divorced from a party member and had joined the Communist Party herself. She was disappointed in communism by the time Oppenheimer met her, but she still remained interested in world affairs. She and Oppenheimer met at a party and were immediately drawn to one another, despite their very different personalities. Kitty admired the brilliant, sensitive scientist. Oppenheimer was charmed by the social, outgoing, vibrant woman. By 1940, the two were married, and in 1941, their son Peter was born.

Oppenheimer was happy with family life and life as a professor. He and Frank bought a ranch together in New Mexico and took their families, friends, and students there for vacations whenever possible. Oppenheimer worried about the growing war in Europe and the Nazi threat, but he was uncertain about how he could help. In September 1941, Lawrence suggested that he join the other physicists in the Uranium

Committee and study the idea of a fission bomb. During his spare time, Oppenheimer began to consider the various theoretical problems involved.

Just three months later, life for all Americans was changed. On December 7, 1941, Japan attacked the American navy at Pearl Harbor, Hawaii, and the United States declared war on the Axis powers. Like everyone in America, Oppenheimer wanted to help his country in the war effort. He, Lawrence, and the other Uranium Committee physicists began to concentrate all their efforts on how nuclear fission might be used in the fight for freedom.

Fission Chain Reactions

One refugee physicist, the Italian Enrico Fermi, was a researcher at the University of Chicago. He experimented with triggering a fission chain reaction. If chain reactions could be created, a fission weapon would become a real possibility. Fermi invented a large machine called an atomic reactor

The Japanese attack on Pearl Harbor drew the United States into World War II, intensifying interest in the use of nuclear fission as a weapon.

Enrico Fermi (center), pictured here with Ernest Lawrence (left), invented the atomic reactor, an important step in developing the atomic bomb.

in which uranium atomic nuclei could be hit by neutrons and split. As a uranium atom split, that atom lost a couple of its own neutrons. These neutrons behaved exactly as the initiating neutrons had. They each shot out and hit more nuclei in other atoms, which split and shot out even more neutrons which hit even more nuclei, on and on, faster and faster, through the uranium pile.

Fermi's chain reaction occurred so fast and so powerfully that his pile of uranium heated up dangerously. Fermi had proved that a chain reaction was possible. The machine that produced the reaction, however, was as big as a building and took 50 tons of uranium. Moreover, no one knew how to make a reliable chain reaction that would explode instead of releasing its energy as heat and radioactivity.

Purifying Uranium

Fermi's chain reaction was fast, but not fast enough to cause an explosion. Part of Fermi's problem was that only some of the atoms in uranium would split easily. He could not control how many atoms split in the chain reaction.

The atoms in natural uranium, like those in all matter, are not completely identical. All uranium atoms have 92 protons and 92 electrons, but uranium atoms can have different numbers of neutrons in their nuclei. These variations of uranium atoms are called isotopes. The isotope called U-238 is the one of which most natural uranium is composed. Less than 1 percent of uranium is the isotope U-235, which has fewer neutrons than U-238. U-235 is more unstable than U-238, and fissions easily. The ratio between U-235 and U-238 in natural uranium can be understood by comparing a chunk of uranium to a rose bush that grows roses of different colors. There would be one hundred red rose isotopes for each single pink rose isotope. If scientists could pick that pink rose, they would be separating the U-235 from the U-238. With a quantity of U-235 purified from natural uranium, there would be fuel for a very fast chain reaction and perhaps a bomb that would explode. Such a chain reaction was named fast fission.

Uranium-235 (pictured) provides fuel for a rapid chain reaction called fast fission, which scientists believed could result in an atomic explosion.

At Columbia University in New York, John Dunning and Eugene Booth were experimenting with purifying uranium by turning it into a gas and filtering the isotopes. This method of trying to separate U-235 from U-238 was called gaseous diffusion. At the same time, Ernest Lawrence realized that he could convert his cyclotron into a machine that accelerated and spun uranium atoms to separate the lighter U-235 from the heavier U-238. He called the process electromagnetic separation because it used electricity and big magnets. Oppenheimer assisted Lawrence in the mathematical theory for the conversion.

Other scientists were experimenting with uranium, too. In 1940, Glenn Seaborg had bombarded uranium and created from it an artificial element that was named plutonium. He made only a speck, but further experiments by Seaborg and others showed plutonium to be so unstable that it fissioned very easily. Physicists thought that it, too, might be a good fuel for a weapon.

Along with the other scientists, Oppenheimer became very excited about the likelihood of a fissioning bomb. He gathered a small group of physicists at Berkeley, and together, they began to figure mathematically the critical mass necessary to make a self-sustaining chain reaction. It was a crucial problem. The critical mass of purified uranium or of plutonium was the exact amount needed to ensure a fast fission chain reaction. If that amount could be determined and assembled, the chain reaction, once begun, should continue on its own, or sustain itself. Critical mass plus a fast fission chain reaction would equal an atomic explosion.

The Manhattan Project Begins

Oppenheimer's group felt pressured to speed their research. The war was not going well for the Allies. In Europe, the Nazis had conquered country after country. In the Pacific, Japan's militarists were gaining great victories. Roosevelt also felt the pressure of war and decided to put his faith in the idea of inventing an atomic bomb in order to achieve victory. In 1942, the government took over all atomic research and put it under military control. The military assigned General

Leslie Groves to direct and run the project. It would be a highly secret, urgent program and have unlimited government funds. The project was code-named the Manhattan Project.

Groves traveled around the country and visited the universities and laboratories where Uranium Committee research was taking place. He was quite disappointed. No one seemed to have a coherent picture of the bomb

The military appointed General Leslie Groves (pictured) to oversee the top secret Manhattan Project, responsible for creating the first atomic bomb.

concept as a whole. The physicists could not or would not explain their results to him in an understandable way. Scientists talked about years of experiments ahead. Sometimes there was enthusiasm about discoveries, but never were there practical results to encourage him. When an actual bomb was mentioned, experimenters considered any such planning to be premature. "We can't just sit on our fannies and meditate!"[5] fumed Groves.

Then, Groves met Oppenheimer. Oppenheimer presented a clear, understandable picture to the general of all the scientific research so far. He explained, in theory, the practical steps that needed to be taken to reach the goal of a working bomb. He described ideas and suggestions for moving the project forward. Groves was so impressed with Oppenheimer and his ability that he took Oppenheimer's advice to build a secret town and laboratories where all the scientists could work together to figure out how to build an atomic bomb. Oppenheimer even knew the perfect place to locate the town—on a remote New Mexico wilderness mesa close to his ranch. Groves chose Oppenheimer to be the administrator and scientific director of the endeavor. He said about Oppenheimer, "He's a genius. A real genius. . . . Why, Oppenheimer knows about everything. He can talk to you about anything you bring up. Well, not exactly. I guess there are a few things he doesn't know about. He doesn't know anything about sports."[6]

Oppenheimer was not interested in sports, but his Communist interests and connections during the 1930s caused concern. He had donated money and time to American Communist Party causes, such as labor unions and racial integration and equality. His wife and brother were former party members. On this basis, some government officials and the FBI objected to Groves's appointment of Oppenheimer. Groves, however, remained firm in his choice and in his faith in Oppenheimer.

> "My two great loves are physics and desert country. It's a pity they can't be combined."
>
> J. ROBERT OPPENHEIMER

Groves had a complete town and factory built in a secret location in Oak Ridge, Tennessee, where purified uranium could be produced. Cyclotrons like Lawrence's, as well as gaseous diffusion equipment modeled after Columbia's, would be used at this plant. Lawrence remained at Berkeley where he could perfect the electromagnetic process and supervise the Oak Ridge work.

Another secret factory and town were built in Hanford, Washington, where physicists led the effort to produce plutonium for a fission bomb. Even though no plutonium or purified uranium had been made yet, work was begun to construct the town and laboratory at the Los Alamos, New Mexico, mesa, where Oppenheimer and his proposed team could design and build an atomic bomb.

Los Alamos Director

Oppenheimer's first task was to assemble his team of scientists. He had to persuade the best and brightest to join him in a secret project that he could not explain to them. Until they agreed to come, he could not even tell them where it was. His reputation and enthusiasm were so great that many scientists packed up their possessions, loaded their families in cars or boarded trains, and quietly disappeared from their homes. Those who had no wives or children had to leave behind their friends and loved ones without any explanation and start over, alone, in the new location. It was a sacrifice most made gladly when they understood how they would help the war effort.

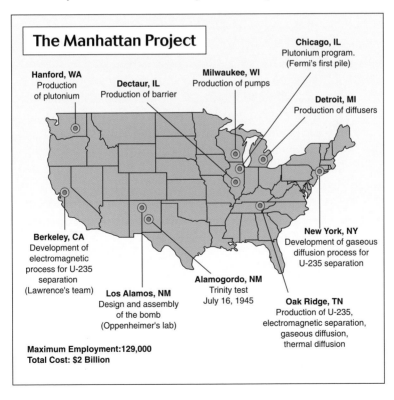

The Manhattan Project

Chicago, IL
Plutonium program.
(Fermi's first pile)

Hanford, WA
Production
of plutonium

Dectaur, IL
Production of barrier

Milwaukee, WI
Production of pumps

Detroit, MI
Production of diffusers

Berkeley, CA
Development of
electromagnetic
process for U-235
separation
(Lawrence's team)

Los Alamos, NM
Design and assembly
of the bomb
(Oppenheimer's lab)

Alamogordo, NM
Trinity test
July 16, 1945

New York, NY
Development of gaseous
diffusion process for
U-235 separation

Oak Ridge, TN
Production of U-235,
electromagnetic separation,
gaseous diffusion,
thermal diffusion

Maximum Employment:129,000
Total Cost: $2 Billion

The European refugees who agreed to come included theoretical physicists Hans Bethe and Edward Teller. Fermi arrived with his family and became the associate director of the project. George Kistiakowsky, an explosives expert, was from Russia and joined Captain William Parsons as a detonation researcher. Even Bohr, who had narrowly escaped the Nazis, came to Los Alamos as a consultant. Frank Oppenheimer joined the project. A group of British scientists, led by Chadwick, came to help. Great American scientists such as the chemist Joseph Kennedy and physicists Robert Bacher, Robert Wilson, Ken Bainbridge, and Seth Neddermeyer lent their talents, as well.

Getting to Work

By the spring of 1943, Oppenheimer and the first arrivals moved to Los Alamos. It was a hastily constructed, primitive place. Living quarters were metal army shelters, barracks, and cheaply built apartments. The heating and cooking stoves never worked properly, and the water faucets often yielded only algae. There were no sidewalks or paved streets. In winter, people slogged through sticky mud and in summer through clouds of dust. Inside the barbed wire that surrounded the town, guarded by military police, scientists would work in their laboratories, children would attend school, couples would relax at parties and dances, doctors would treat the sick, and families would remain until the bomb work had succeeded.

When Oppenheimer and his scientists gathered for their first meeting, workmen were still hammering in the building. Since their meeting could be overheard, Oppenheimer told the scientists to say "gadget," not "bomb," and the nickname stuck. At that first meeting, they discussed what research had been done already, what questions and problems needed to be addressed before they could build the gadget, and what kind of deadlines they would set for themselves.

Oppenheimer also announced that they would have to build two types of gadgets. One would be a design for a possible uranium bomb; the other would be for a plutonium

A scientist sits next to Oppenheimer's gadget, a nickname he used for the first atomic bomb to protects its secrecy.

bomb. Since no one knew which would be workable, they would have to be prepared for whatever fuel was produced. Neither Oak Ridge nor Hanford would be able to supply them with enough U-235 or plutonium for at least two years. Oppenheimer said that they could not wait for the fuel to arrive and then experiment to see if a bomb could be built. When the fuel was ready, they had to be ready to insert it into a bomb and immediately ship it overseas to the war front.

Any delay might mean that the Nazi scientists developed an atom bomb first. Even a day's delay meant the loss of more American soldiers' lives. All the scientists felt the urgency of their task. They would have regular meetings to discuss their progress.

Four Divisions, Many Tasks

Oppenheimer was the scientific leader as well as the administrator of Los Alamos. He divided his scientists into four divisions, each with a division leader and each with specific tasks. The Theoretical Physics Division was headed by Bethe. It was this group's responsibility to finish mathematically figuring the final critical mass of U-235 and plutonium. They had to determine how large an atomic bomb explosion would be, how much destruction it might cause, and how much radioactivity would be released. They also tried to predict how damaging radioactivity would be to people, although not much was known about its effects.

The dangers of radioactivity from unstable atoms had been known for years. Natural radioactivity in subatomic particle streams penetrates all kinds of matter, even people. When these particle streams penetrate cells in the human body, those cells are disrupted and damaged. Repeated exposure to radioactivity over time can kill. No one knew, however, how much more intense the radioactivity would be from purified uranium or plutonium or how damaging it would be when released in great quantity in an explosion.

The Experimental Physics Division was extremely cautious about handling radioactive material. This division was led by Bacher. He and his team were responsible for the actual experiments that had to be done with plutonium and U-235. Since no one knew how far neutrons had to travel before they caused fission, the experimental physicists had to count the number of neutrons released with each fission, where the neutrons went, and the length of time between each fission.

They also needed to figure the kind of tamper materials that would surround the fuel. Without a tamper, many of the neutrons released in a chain reaction would go flying off into the air. The tamper would have to stop these neutrons and reflect them back into the chain reaction so that it could proceed even faster.

The Chemical and Metallurgical Division was headed by Kennedy. Since the plutonium arrived from Hanford in a soft, syrupy state, this group had to learn to turn the plutonium back into a metal that could be molded and shaped as needed for the bomb.

Parsons headed the Ordnance Division. He was a navy officer and an expert in explosives. His division developed the actual shape of the bomb and made sure it could fit in an airplane.

The Trusted Leader

Oppenheimer kept up with the work of all four divisions, ready to step in if there was a problem. He kept a picture of all the work and problems in his mind. Daily, he read reports from the divisions and sent reports of his own to Groves. Every scientist knew that Oppenheimer considered his work of vital importance and appreciated his efforts. Oppenheimer became not just leader, but friend, father figure, and mentor to his scientific teams. He led discussion groups, encouraged his scientists, soothed his discouraged team members, and coordinated everyone's research. Many of the scientists had big egos and were not used to working as a team. Oppenheimer eased hurt feelings and arguments. When Teller insisted on doing his own independent research, for example, Oppenheimer set him up on his own and held regular meetings with him about his progress.

Oppenheimer became a skilled leader on the Manhattan Project. The above photograph is taken from his identification badge.

Oppenheimer did his best to solve all Los Alamos problems, both big and small. One physicist kept speeding in his car despite complaints and warnings from the Los Alamos traffic safety committee Oppenheimer had instituted. The committee levied fines, but the scientist refused to pay them. Oppenheimer called the physicist in to his office and firmly said, "Owen Chamberlain, it's time for you to put up or shut up. You ought to pay that fine."[7] Chamberlain paid.

Oppenheimer was a leader who cared about everyone, not just his scientists. He learned the names of hundreds of people at Los Alamos and tried to form a relationship with each one. With one pregnant woman, he sympathized about the difficulties of pregnancy during the hot summer months. He gave fatherly advice to couples who got married at Los Alamos. When babies were born, he visited and congratulated the parents. Many native New Mexicans worked to help the scientists run the town of Los Alamos. Oppenheimer stopped in the street to greet them and let them know they were appreciated. One janitor bragged that he and "Oppie" were such good friends that he could spit on the director's floor without getting in trouble.

> "Here, at great expense, the government has assembled the world's largest collection of crackpots."
>
> GENERAL LESLIE GROVES

Oppenheimer seemed to be everywhere and to handle any kind of problem, but scientific problems occupied most of his time. When an experiment seemed stalled, Oppenheimer would listen to the problem and then suggest a new pathway to try. When a group suffered a setback in its research, Oppenheimer thought of new ideas to get them going again. Always, he was available to listen to a new idea and approve new research that might prove valuable. The arrogance and snobbery of his youth were gone. He was gentle, supportive, and kind in his leadership. And he was diplomatic in his dealings with the military.

The Demands of Leadership

Groves sometimes telephoned four or five times a day. He wanted results and did not care how complicated bomb design problems were. Daily, Oppenheimer reassured Groves and kept him from harassing the scientists. Some problems, though, Oppenheimer could not solve for the demanding general. Groves thought that too many babies were being born at Los Alamos, which cost the project too much money. He wanted Oppenheimer to put a stop to it. Oppenheimer made no such effort. His own daughter, Toni, was born at Los Alamos in 1944.

For the most part, Oppenheimer and Groves had a good relationship. Oppenheimer respected the general and turned to him for anything the project needed. Groves knew how important Oppenheimer was to the success of Los Alamos and tried to protect him and keep him from working too hard.

Groves was so determined to keep Oppenheimer safe that he restricted what Oppenheimer was allowed to do. In July 1943, he sent Oppenheimer a letter that read:

Groves and Oppenheimer met regularly while at Los Alamos and had a good working relationship.

Dear Dr. Oppenheimer,

In view of the nature of the work on which you are engaged, the knowledge of it which is possessed by you and the dependence which rests upon you for its successful accomplishment, it seems necessary to ask you to take certain special precautions with respect to your personal safety.

It is requested that:

(a) You refrain from flying in airplanes of any description; the time saved is not worth the risk. (If emergency demands their use my prior consent should be requested.)

(b) You refrain from driving an automobile for any appreciable distance (above a few miles) and from being without suitable protection on any lonely road, such as the road from Los Alamos to Santa Fe. On such trips you should be accompanied by a competent, able bodied, armed guard. There is no objection to the guard serving as a chauffeur.

(c) Your cars be driven with due regard to safety and that in driving about town a guard of some kind should be used, particularly during hours of darkness. The cost of such guard is a proper charge against the United States.

I realize that these precautions may be personally burdensome and that they may appear to you to be unduly restrictive but I am asking you to bear with them until our work is successfully completed.

Sincerely,

L.R. Groves

Brigadier General, C.E.[8]

Oppenheimer accepted calmly all the restrictions on his freedom. He knew they were necessary during wartime. Kitty Oppenheimer, however, did not accept Los Alamos life very easily. She was unhappy living behind barbed wire and began to drink heavily. She often insisted on shopping trips to California and left the two children with sitters and nannies. Oppenheimer was too wrapped up in his work to pay much attention to Kitty or the children. His neglect was sad for his family but part of the sacrifice he made for the project.

Oppenheimer worked with intense concentration and motivation. Not unusual for him were 18- and 20-hour workdays. His dedication inspired his teams of physicists to labor just as hard. Many referred to themselves proudly as Oppie's Army. Groves had installed a military siren that went off at seven each morning to start the workday. The scientists called it Oppie's Whistle, and they hurried to their laboratories when they heard it, sure that Oppenheimer was already at work.

Some mathematical research and experiments, especially those that involved the movements of neutrons, had to be worked on for months before a solution could be found.

Unhappy with life in Los Alamos, Kitty Oppenheimer often left her two children with sitters for shopping trips in California.

Once, some physicists had worked and argued all day over a set of figures on the blackboard. Oppenheimer came in, listened quietly, stared at the board, then changed a small set of figures, and silently departed. The physicists' problem had been solved. With such insights, Oppenheimer earned the respect of his scientists.

Bethe once said about Oppenheimer,

> He knew and understood everything that went on in the laboratory, whether it was chemistry or theoretical physics or machine shop. He could keep it all in his head and coordinate it. It was clear also at Los Alamos that he was superior to us. He understood immediately when he heard anything, and fitted it into the general scheme of things and drew the right conclusions. There was just no one else in that laboratory who even came close to him. In his knowledge.[9]

Solutions and Problems

By the summer of 1944, the Los Alamos scientists knew how much fuel was needed and had built models of each type of bomb. To trigger the bomb's chain reaction, they had settled on a gun method. They would separate the critical mass into two subcritical masses. One subcritical mass would be the bullet. It would be shot at high speed at the other subcritical mass. This gun method smashed the two masses together in thousandths of a second so that the mass became critical, and a fast fission chain reaction occurred in a millionth of a second. The gun barrel for the bomb had been invented, and the tampers were in place. The shape of the bomb and its size had been settled.

Then the experimental physicists discovered a crushing problem. Small samples of plutonium had been arriving from Hanford, and the experimental physicists had performed more than two thousand experiments on them. They discovered that the gun method would work for U-235, but not for plutonium. Plutonium is so unstable that neutrons often shot out of it spontaneously. The gun method could not assemble the subcritical masses fast enough. Too many neutrons would shoot out by themselves before the chain reaction was started properly, and the bomb would melt down and fail.

The discovery was a dreadful blow for Oppenheimer. He had put all his faith and efforts into the gun method. If it would not work for the plutonium bomb, he believed his error in judgment was so big that he was a failure as the leader of the project. He considered abandoning the plutonium bomb altogether. He even considered resigning, but Bacher persuaded him that there was no one else who could take his place. At last, with much worry, Oppenheimer decided that they would try a new method that had been proposed by Neddermeyer. It was called implosion, and it had never been done before.

Implosion

Implosion meant blowing explosives inward toward a ball of plutonium. If the shock waves of the detonation squeezed the plutonium ball perfectly evenly, the ball would become a walnut-sized critical mass, and fast fission would occur. No neutrons could escape prematurely. Oppenheimer reorganized laboratory efforts, created a new Gadget Division, and set every available scientist to work on the problem. The chances

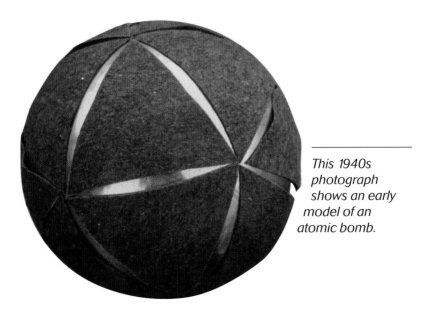

This 1940s photograph shows an early model of an atomic bomb.

Because fuel was in short supply for the Little Boy uranium bomb (above), only the Fat Man plutonium bomb (below right) was tested at the Trinity site.

that implosion would work seemed small, but Oppenheimer encouraged Neddermeyer and promised him a bottle of whiskey if he succeeded.

Implosion was so difficult that few thought it could be done. Month after month, explosions could be heard on the mesa as different explosive experiments were tried. Always, they failed. The scientists could not squeeze or compress anything completely evenly. Bulges, rips, bubbles, and twists would appear in the balls, pipes, and beer cans that they detonated. Bulges meant uneven compression. Too many neutrons would have escaped in the wrong direction if the items used in the explosive experiments had been real plutonium bombs. Uneven compression would not do for plutonium. A fast fission chain reaction depended on the critical mass being assembled all at once, in a millionth of a second.

Finally, after a year of work, a solution was found. The core of plutonium would be separated into two hemispheres and surrounded by a series of reflecting lenses that sat inside a shell. When a conventional explosive detonated the bomb, the shock wave from the explosion would be reflected, curved, and directed evenly by the lenses. This shock wave would then smoothly compress the ball of plutonium inward until a critical mass was reached. An initiator at the center of the ball would melt from the heat as the shock wave reached it. The initiator would release a neutron stream and begin the plutonium's fast fission chain reaction. It was incredibly complex, but all of Los Alamos hoped it would work.

Little Boy and Fat Man

By 1945, both the Oak Ridge plant and the Hanford plant were able to produce the needed quantity of U-235 and plutonium. Los Alamos was ready to build two bombs. The uranium bomb was nicknamed Little Boy because its casing was sleek, and its detonation was simple. The plutonium bomb, with its complicated ignition process, was round and awkward looking. It was called Fat Man.

There was enough fuel to make only one uranium bomb, so Little Boy could not be tested. Besides, the design of Little Boy made the scientists reasonably sure that it would work if Fat Man did. Oppenheimer insisted that Fat Man had to be tested. Enough plutonium was arriving from Hanford that a twin to Fat Man could be built. Groves was upset at the delay, but Oppenheimer said that the bomb was so complex that a test was absolutely necessary. He wrote a memorandum that explained, "If we do *not* have accurate test data from Trinity, the planning of use of the gadget over enemy territory will have to be done substantially blindly." [10]

Preparing for the Test

Trinity was the code name that Oppenheimer had chosen for the site where Fat Man would be tested. Groves and Oppenheimer selected the site. It was a barren stretch of desert in a

corner of the air force's Alamogordo Bombing Range in New Mexico. Oppenheimer chose the code name from a favorite poem by John Donne. In the spring of 1945, Oppenheimer assigned a group of scientists, led by Bainbridge, to move to the site and supervise its preparation. Groves brought in a military force to construct and guard it.

The Fat Man replica would sit at the top of a 100-foot steel tower at ground zero. Bunkers and observation posts were built around ground zero, both to protect the observers and to provide a place for scientific instruments. The south shelter was the command shelter, about 5.5 miles away from the tower. The north and west shelters were also about 5.5 miles from ground zero and would hold cameras, searchlights, and various recording instruments. All three were bunkers dug into the earth with roofs of concrete. At the base camp, about 10 miles away from the tower, trenches were dug so that observers could lie in them and observe the test outside. Another observation point, Compania Hill, was 20 miles away. Here, the Los Alamos scientists not needed at Trinity, as well as a few select visitors, would be allowed to watch the test.

In May 1945, Germany was defeated by the Allied forces. The Manhattan Project learned that the Nazis had never been close to building an atomic bomb. The Nazi scientists had taken a wrong direction in their research. Arguments, jealousies, and competition had stalled their efforts altogether. A few scientists in the Manhattan Project wanted to stop America's effort to build a bomb now that Germany was no longer a threat, but the war in the Pacific still raged, fierce and bloody. Roosevelt had died. Harry Truman, the new president, decided that the United States would use the bomb to end the fighting with Japan if the Trinity test was successful.

At the Trinity Site

Oppenheimer selected a test date of July 16, 1945. On July 10, he sent a coded telegram to his good friend, Lawrence, to invite him to witness the test. It read, "Any time after the 15th would be good for our fishing trip. Because we are not certain of the weather, we may be delayed several days. We do not have enough sleeping bags to go around, so we ask you please not to bring anyone with you."[11]

Fat Man was driven carefully from Los Alamos to Trinity. It was gently raised to the top of the tower with winches. Once the bomb was safely in place, it was connected by wires and cables to the arming switches and various test instruments in the shelters. Some of the wiring was strung along telephone poles and cacti. Some was threaded through garden hose and laid along the ground.

On the evening of July 15, Oppenheimer climbed alone to the top of the tower to look at Fat Man once more. All was in readiness, and his work was finished. No one knew what he felt or thought as he gazed that last time at the result of all his labors.

In the desert, where rain was unusual, thunderstorms threatened to ruin the test that night. Groves growled at the weather forecasters. Some scientists suggested delaying the test. Tense and worried, Oppenheimer decided to wait and see. He stayed awake all night, paced the floor, chain-smoked, coughed, and agonized. He feared that either the test would

---

Fat Man, like this test bomb, was driven to the test site and winched into place.

be ruined by the weather or the bomb would fizzle altogether. He was so concerned about the success of the test that everyone could see how nervous he was. Frank tried to comfort and reassure his brother. Kistiakowsky bet him a month's salary against ten dollars that the bomb would work. Oppenheimer smiled a little but did not calm down.

As the night wound down, the storms finally passed, and the sky began to clear. Oppenheimer chose a 5:30 A.M. detonation time, and all the scientists went to their assigned places. Groves went to base camp and lay down in one of the protective trenches with other observers. Oppenheimer remained in the command shelter with the physicist who would throw the last arming switch and broadcast the countdown. Even on Compania Hill, 20 miles away, all the observers who were outside wore dark, thick welder's glasses to protect their eyes from the expected bomb flash. The countdown began.

Success

At exactly 5:29:45 A.M., before dawn on July 16, the bomb was detonated. The resulting explosion far surpassed Oppenheimer's most optimistic expectations. Kistiakowsky had not been willing to stay in the command shelter, but stood on its roof. When the shock wave hit him, he was thrown off the roof and fell to the ground. He leaped up and, as Oppenheimer emerged from the shelter, joyfully threw muddy arms around him. "Oppie, Oppie! I won the bet, you owe me $10!"[12] Kistiakowsky shouted. Oppenheimer trembled and embraced Kistiakowsky in relief. At all the observation posts,

"There are people who say they are not such very bad weapons. Before the New Mexico test we sometimes said that, too, writing down square miles and equivalent tonnages and looking at the pictures of ravaged Europe. After the test we did not say that anymore."
J. ROBERT OPPENHEIMER

excitement and congratulations erupted. The sight of the first atomic bomb explosion was awe inspiring, overwhelming, and never to be forgotten. Uppermost in everyone's mind was intense relief that Fat Man had worked.

No such explosion had ever been witnessed or even imagined. The steel tower was completely vaporized. The sand at its base was melted into a green glasslike substance. In the north and west shelters, at the moment of detonation, instruments

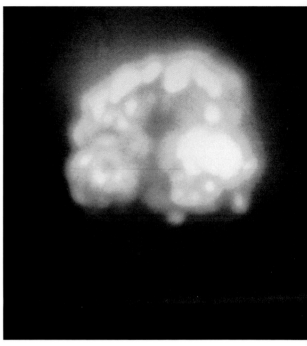

The explosion of the world's first atomic bomb blew out windows 235 miles away.

seemed to go dead. For a moment, the physicists stared at their recording instruments and feared the test had failed, but the readings for the bomb's explosive force had simply gone off the scale. On Compania Hill, one physicist had removed his protective glasses, sure that he was too far away to suffer any damage. The initial flash completely blinded him for about 30 seconds, even from 20 miles away. Windows blew out of buildings in Gallup, New Mexico, 235 miles away from Trinity.

At base camp, Fermi measured the size of the blast. When the shock wave hit him, he dribbled bits of paper from his hand and watched how far they blew in the wind. From the distance they traveled, he estimated the size of the blast at 20,000 tons of TNT, 2,000 times the biggest conventional bomb in use in the war.

47

Oppenheimer and Groves (center) inspect the remains of the 100-foot steel bomb tower.

Oppenheimer climbed into a car and rode back to base camp. Groves greeted him with solemn congratulations, and Oppenheimer quietly thanked him. For the first time in months, Oppenheimer visibly relaxed. He stood with confidence and pride. He had accomplished what he had set out to do, and he had justified Groves's faith in him. Groves was thrilled with the impressive success of the test. He left to inform Washington that the United States now had two atomic bombs to be used against Japan.

Then Bainbridge approached Oppenheimer. They clasped hands, and Bainbridge said softly, "Now we're all sons-of-bitches."[13] Oppenheimer felt that was the best comment anybody made about the atomic bomb test. The scientists had conquered the atom, but their great achievement would cause horrific death and destruction. The joy of success was wearing off. Oppenheimer got into a jeep and rode up into the hills as the mushroom cloud drifted harmlessly off into the distance. He walked in the desert that had always been his place to find peace. Close to the bomb site, every bit of life was destroyed, but as Oppenheimer walked, he came upon a turtle that had been thrown onto its back by the shock wave.

Alive and kicking, the turtle struggled futilely to right itself. Oppenheimer bent over and gently set the animal on its feet. He watched it scurry away, glad that he could help one small living thing.

Hiroshima and Nagasaki

Days later Little Boy and another Fat Man were shipped overseas and handed over to the U.S. Army Air Force. On August 6, 1945, Little Boy was dropped on Hiroshima, Japan. On August 9, Fat Man was dropped on Nagasaki. Japan sued for peace the next day. The atomic bomb drops were announced to the public, and the secret Manhattan Project was revealed to the world. Throughout America, elation and joy erupted. The war was over. No more American soldiers would have to die. And the Manhattan Project scientists were the heroes who had won the war.

Military inspectors examine the destruction left by the atomic bomb dropped on Hiroshima, Japan. The war with Japan ended after America dropped a second bomb on Nagasaki.

TIME
THE WEEKLY NEWSMAGAZINE

PHYSICIST OPPENHEIMER
"What we don't understand, we explain to each other."
(*Education*)

Although magazines such as Time *featured him on their covers and he became a celebrity, Oppenheimer grew depressed over the use of the bomb.*

At Los Alamos, the initial reaction to the bombing was one of triumph and happiness, too. When Oppenheimer announced the successful use of Little Boy, there were cheers, but by the time peace was declared, a different reaction had set in. Many Los Alamos scientists were unable to celebrate the end of the war. All they could think of were the Japanese deaths that their work had caused. In Hiroshima, 140,000 people died. In Nagasaki, 78,000 more were killed. On the evening the scientists tried to have a victory party, Oppenheimer found a young physicist vomiting in the bushes. As he comforted the distressed scientist, Oppenheimer thought that this weapon of terror had to be turned into good. It had to be used to convince the world that war was no longer possible.

Oppenheimer found himself a celebrity with the general public and one of the most admired people in America and in Europe. Newspaper reporters interviewed him, and his picture was on the covers of *Life* and *Time* magazines. He was described as the dashing, eloquent genius who had guided the creation of the atomic bomb. He cooperated graciously with the press, but all the accolades did not help his growing depression over the use of the bomb. Along with Kitty and the children, he retreated to his New Mexico ranch, where he could escape public attention and find peace. He spent quiet evenings playing by the fireplace with his children. He went for leisurely walks with Kitty to search for four-leaf clovers. He took long horseback rides through his beloved wilderness and let the natural beauty heal his distress.

Mothers of soldiers wrote grateful letters of thanks that found their way to him, and these letters cheered him. His depression over the horrible effects of the bomb was helped most by a letter he received from a soldier in the Pacific. The soldier had been one of Oppenheimer's students and had been waiting for invasion orders that were now canceled by Japan's surrender. The brief letter read, "Hey, Oppie, you're about the best loved man in these parts."[14]

Oppenheimer did not regret his role in the development of the bomb, but he did feel a profound determination that it should never be used again, and he was tired. Like many others in the Manhattan Project, he decided to leave Los Alamos and return to peaceful university life. On his last day as director, October 16, 1945, he gave a speech to his fellow scientists in which he talked about his hopes for a new world. He expressed his belief that a weapon had been created that was so powerful that war should now be impossible. Always, in the past, when people had hoped a powerful new weapon would put an end to war, their hopes had been in vain, but this time, Oppenheimer insisted, all those responsible for the atom bomb had to make these hopes come true. He said,

> If atomic bombs are to be added as new weapons to the arsenals of a warring world, or

"What has been done is the greatest achievement of organized science in history. It has been done under high pressure and without failure. We have spent two billion dollars on the greatest scientific gamble in history—and won."

PRESIDENT HARRY TRUMAN

to the arsenals of nations preparing for war, then the time will come when mankind will curse the names of Los Alamos and Hiroshima.

The peoples of the world must unite, or they will perish. This war, that has ravaged so much of the earth, has written these words. The atomic bomb has spelled them out for all men to understand. Other men have spoken them, in other times, of other wars, of other weapons. They have not prevailed. There are some, misled by a false sense of human history, who hold that they will not prevail today. It is not for us to believe that. By our works, we are committed, committed to a world united, before the common peril, in law, and in humanity.[15]

After Los Alamos

Oppenheimer never again worked in nuclear bomb research. He accepted a directorship at Princeton University's Institute of Advanced Study where he could return to teaching and explore theoretical ideas with his colleagues. He also became a scientific adviser to the government and tried to influence political decisions about the use of nuclear energy. He was the most admired scientist in the country, and many government officials listened to and trusted his opinions.

"By taking thought of our often grim responsibility, by knowing something of our profound and omnipresent imperfection, we may help our children's children to a world less cruel, perhaps less unjust, less likely to end in catastrophe beyond words. We may even find our way to put an end to the orgy, the killing, the brutality that is war."

J. ROBERT OPPENHEIMER

The Scientist Statesman

At Oppenheimer's urging, the U.S. government established an Atomic Energy Commission with a General Advisory Committee (GAC) of scientists to guide the future of Los Alamos and nuclear research. This was a significant accomplishment because it took atomic research out of military control and removed it from military secrecy. Oppenheimer was selected to serve on the GAC and was elected to be its chairman.

As the GAC chairman, Oppenheimer began a new phase in his life as a scientist statesman. He wielded a great deal of power and influenced government policies about atomic bombs and nuclear research. His insistent efforts to promote peaceful uses of atomic power made him many enemies. The military wanted more bombs, more powerful bombs, and further weapons research. Some physicists were anxious to continue the weapons work, also. Teller, who had researched the possibility of a "superbomb," the hydrogen bomb, at Los Alamos, was a strong believer in building better atomic bombs. Lawrence believed that if America did not build a hydrogen bomb, Soviet Russia would do it first and endanger the whole free world. He tried to persuade the government to support a new laboratory devoted to superbombs. Some people in government believed that all nuclear research and knowledge should remain exclusively in American hands.

Oppenheimer and the other scientists on the GAC fought all these proposals and recommended against them. Oppenheimer believed that scientific openness was the only pathway to permanent peace. He wanted all atomic knowledge freely shared and research internationally controlled, so that no one nation could engender fear and suspicion in other nations with secret weapons. For several years, Oppenheimer was successful in his efforts to prevent secrecy about atomic energy, to discourage the building of the hydrogen bomb, and to avoid a worldwide nuclear arms race. Many in government and most physicists appreciated his moral stands, agreed with his beliefs, and supported him. The military, however, came to distrust Oppenheimer. Teller was angry at his refusal to support plans for the superbomb. Lawrence turned against his old friend and thought his political power had made him arrogant.

Cold War Fears

World events soon worked in favor of Oppenheimer's critics. In 1949, Soviet Russia exploded an atomic device of its own.

In 1952, the Soviets exploded a hydrogen bomb. The United States was no longer the world's only atomic power. Although America finally did build Teller's superbomb, also in 1952, many in the United States felt threatened and angry at Oppenheimer for holding up scientific development of atomic weapons. An arms race began between the United States and the Soviets. Worldwide destruction and nuclear annihilation become possible.

People in government began to look on Oppenheimer with suspicion and dislike. One government official brought charges before the Atomic Energy Commission that Oppenheimer was disloyal, a danger to the United States, and a Soviet spy who had stalled American bomb development so

A mushroom cloud rises from a Pacific atoll in the first U.S. test of a hydrogen bomb. Oppenheimer's stand against weapons such as this angered many in the government.

the Soviets could catch up. Conservative members of the Atomic Energy Commission, led by Admiral Lewis Strauss, seized on these charges to attack Oppenheimer and force him out of government.

Security Risk

The Atomic Energy Commission brought formal charges against Oppenheimer in December 1953. They accused him of being a security risk who could not be trusted with America's scientific secrets. Everyone who worked for the government had to have security clearance. This meant that the FBI checked their background, current behavior, and beliefs. People trusted to be loyal Americans and keep American secrets were given security clearance. Oppenheimer's security clearance was suspended until a hearing could be held to judge him on the charges. With his clearance suspended, Oppenheimer was not allowed to see secret papers that he had actually written himself.

When the charges were read to him, Oppenheimer was stunned and numb. He could not understand how this could be happening to him after his years of loyal, patriotic service. It was a heavy blow, but he made up his mind to fight the charges.

The Trial

The Atomic Energy Commission appointed a three-member board to conduct an inquiry into the charges and to rule on whether Oppenheimer's security clearance should be revoked. It was supposed to be a relaxed, informal inquiry, but it did not turn out that way. Very soon, the inquiry became a harsh, adversarial trial. The board chose a prosecuting attorney to present the evidence and to interrogate Oppenheimer. The prosecution witnesses testified that Oppenheimer had too many Communist ties during the 1930s to be trusted in the 1950s. They claimed that he showed poor judgment in his refusal to support development of the hydrogen bomb. They complained that too many physicists at Los Alamos became pacifists and that this was Oppenheimer's fault. They argued that Oppenheimer was disloyal in his failure to show enthusiasm for the hydrogen bomb and for military uses of nuclear energy. Teller testified that Oppenheimer had too much influence over other scientists and hurt scientific research.

In Oppenheimer's defense, thirty witnesses testified to his loyalty, his patriotism, and his service to his country. Even Groves testified on Oppenheimer's behalf. Some physicists loudly expressed their outrage at the angry, prejudiced treatment Oppenheimer was getting. All these efforts were useless.

The Verdict

The board ruled that Oppenheimer was discreet, could keep secrets, and showed no indication of disloyalty or Communist involvement. Then they ruled two to one that Oppenheimer's security clearance should be revoked. They pronounced him arrogant and guilty of ideas and opinions that had hurt the national defense and slowed the development of America's nuclear arsenal. The Atomic Energy Commission accepted the verdict, revoked Oppenheimer's security clearance, and ended his work in government. Strauss declared that Oppenheimer was unfit to serve his country.

Although many thoughtful people believed the verdict made a mockery of justice, many others were suspicious of Oppenheimer for the rest of his life. For a time, Oppenheimer was a broken man who felt that his life had been destroyed. Many friends, however, rallied around him. Kitty and the children fiercely defended him. Oppenheimer had not lost his Princeton job, so he returned there and tried to pick up the pieces of his life.

Oppenheimer's Princeton years were quiet, but fulfilling.

He spent more time with his wife and growing children. He was an admired and respected director who attracted gifted students and researchers to the university. His old university friend, Dirac, was there, and Oppenheimer and Dirac renewed their relationship. He also traveled throughout America and the world and gave speeches to appreciative audiences about philosophy, knowledge, education, science, and peace. He acquired a new sailboat and became again the skilled sailor of his youth. He never expressed bitterness in public about what had happened to him with the government.

Redemption

By 1963, the U.S. government had become influenced by more liberal thought than in the 1950s. Many influential people wanted to reverse the unfairness of Oppenheimer's ouster from government. Before President John F. Kennedy died, he selected Oppenheimer to receive a prestigious award for scientific contributions to the country. It was known as the Fermi Award, named in honor of Enrico Fermi, who had died of cancer. Oppenheimer was presented the award in the White House by President Lyndon Johnson. The award citation read, "To J. Robert Oppenheimer for his contributions to theoretical physics as a teacher and originator of ideas and for leadership of the atomic energy program during critical years."[16]

Oppenheimer was touched and very grateful for the award. The approval of his scientific colleagues and the appreciation of his country were meaningful and important to him, but he refused to try to regain his security clearance, as some old friends suggested. He had had enough of politics and would put himself through no more battles. He was contented with his quiet Princeton life.

> "What he believed in, he held to. He willingly exchanged his victor's laurel for a crown of martyrdom."
>
> STAN ULAM, MATHEMATICIAN

Physics Loses Its Genius

In 1966, Oppenheimer was diagnosed with cancer of the throat, and, for a year, underwent radiation treatment in the hope of a remission or cure. He was proud to be using a treatment based on peaceful uses of nuclear energy. The cancer could not be stopped, however, and Oppenheimer grew gravely ill. He showed his determination and bravery to the last and did not complain. "I have to die some year, and mine has been a pretty good life,"[17] he said.

On February 18, 1967, Robert Oppenheimer died at the age of sixty-two. His funeral was attended by six hundred people, and his death was mourned all over the world. His funeral was a reunion of old Los Alamos friends and colleagues. Oppenheimer would always be remembered there with love, friendship, and gratitude.

Bethe was one of the speakers at the service. He said, "J. Robert Oppenheimer did more than any other man to make American physics great. . . . His was a truly brilliant mind, best described by his long-time associate Charles Lauritsen: 'This man . . . always gave you the answer before you had time to formulate the question.'"[18]

Said Henry DeWolf Smyth from the Atomic Energy Commission, "We hope he knew how greatly his country and the world have been rewarded by his work."[19]

Kitty Oppenheimer and Frank carried Oppenheimer's ashes to the ocean and scattered them over the waters he had loved to sail.

The Nuclear Age

Oppenheimer once said, "It is a profound and necessary truth that the deep things in science are not found because they are useful; they are found because it was possible to find them."[20] Because it was possible, the atomic bomb would have been developed sometime by some group in some country. Oppenheimer's leadership at Los Alamos ensured that the United States developed the bomb and was able to shorten World War II. Most people are grateful that it was the United States that developed the first atomic bomb and not some other country.

This statue of J. Robert Oppenheimer greets visitors at the Bradbury Science Museum in Los Alamos, New Mexico. The museum honors the man and his genius.

The atomic explosion at Trinity marked the beginning of the nuclear age. Nuclear weapons that threaten the very existence of the planet are one legacy of the Manhattan Project. When Oppenheimer is remembered, the fearsomeness of nuclear weapons is also remembered. Oppenheimer feared a nuclear war, but that fear has not been realized. He hoped that his work would lead to nuclear energy used as a benefit to humanity, and that has happened.

Today, Los Alamos is the national laboratory for U.S. nuclear research. Its mission is to apply science and engineering to solve problems of national security. Part of the laboratory's work still involves nuclear weapons research, but much of the research is devoted to peaceful uses of nuclear energy and scientific discoveries. The laboratory works on nuclear energy for power, nuclear science for medicine, and has even developed bacteria that digest TNT to help the environment.

The Bradbury Science Museum in Los Alamos welcomes visitors to its exhibits about the Manhattan Project and the laboratory's first director, J. Robert Oppenheimer. At Los Alamos, the father of the atomic bomb is remembered with pride, respect, and admiration.

IMPORTANT DATES

1904	J. Robert Oppenheimer is born.
1912	Frank Oppenheimer is born.
1921	Robert graduates from high school.
1925	Robert graduates from Harvard.
1927	Oppenheimer receives his PhD in physics from the University of Göttingen.
1929	Oppenheimer accepts a dual professorship at the University of California at Berkeley and at the California Institute of Technology.
1939	The fissioning of the uranium atom is announced. World War II begins in Europe with the Nazi invasion of Poland.
1940	Oppenheimer marries Kitty Harrison.
1941	Oppenheimer's son Peter is born.
	Oppenheimer joins the Uranium Committee work.
	Pearl Harbor is attacked and the United States enters World War II.
1942	The Manhattan Project begins with General Leslie Groves as the military director.
	Oppenheimer is appointed scientific director and administrator of Los Alamos.
1943	Oppenheimer and his family move to Los Alamos.
1944	Oppenheimer's daughter Toni is born.
1945	Germany is defeated by the Allies.
	The first atomic bomb is successfully detonated at Trinity.
	Little Boy is dropped on Hiroshima, Japan.
	Fat Man is dropped on Nagasaki, Japan.
	Victory in Japan. World War II ends.
	Oppenheimer resigns as director of Los Alamos.
1947	Oppenheimer accepts the position of director at the Institute for Advanced Study, Princeton, New Jersey.
1954	Oppenheimer's security clearance as a scientific adviser to the U.S. government is revoked.
1963	Oppenheimer receives the Enrico Fermi Award from President Lyndon B. Johnson.
1966	Oppenheimer is diagnosed with throat cancer and begins treatment.
1967	Oppenheimer dies at home in Princeton, New Jersey.

GLOSSARY

atom: The basic building block of all matter. An atom consists of protons, neutrons, and electrons. A nucleus at the center of the atom holds the protons and neutrons. Electrons orbit the nucleus.

chain reaction: A cascade reaction caused by atomic fission in which two or more neutrons are released, fly out at high speed, and hit and split other nuclei which release more neutrons, and so on. The result of this multiplying number of fissions is a self-sustaining chain reaction.

critical mass: The exact amount of fissionable material required to produce a self-sustaining chain reaction.

cyclotron: A particle accelerator. With large magnets and electricity, atoms are accelerated and spun, either to break them apart or to separate those of different weights from one another.

electron: A subatomic particle that orbits the nucleus at the center of the atom. It has a negative electrical charge.

fission: The splitting of the nucleus of an atom.

implosion: An explosion that moves inward rather than blowing outward.

isotopes: The atoms of the same kind of matter, like uranium, that have the same number of electrons and protons, but do not have the same number of neutrons as other atoms of the substance.

neutron: A subatomic particle that provides stability and contributes weight in the atom. Neutrons are in the nucleus of the atom and have no electrical charge.

nucleus: The central part of the atom. *Nuclei* is plural.

proton: A subatomic particle in the nucleus of the atom. A proton carries a positive electrical charge.

quantum theory: The explanation of the behavior and essential character of atomic energy and subatomic particles. Energy is defined as a wave of discrete energy packets known as quanta, or bits of energy.

radioactivity: A subatomic particle stream produced from the nucleus of an unstable atom as it decays or fissions.

tamper: The material that surrounds a critical mass of fissioning fuel and reflects stray neutrons back into the chain reaction.

U-235: The isotope of natural uranium with only 143 neutrons in its nucleus. U-235 is very unstable and fissions easily.

U-238: The isotope of natural uranium with 146 neutrons in its nucleus. Its atoms are stable and do not fission easily.

FOR MORE INFORMATION

BOOKS

J. E. Driemen, *Atomic Dawn: A Biography of Robert Oppenheimer* (People in Focus). Minneapolis, MN: Dillon, 1989.

Doreen Gonzales, *The Manhattan Project and the Atomic Bomb*. Berkeley Heights, NJ: Enslow, 2000.

Tom Seddon, *Atom Bomb* (Scientific American Books for Young Readers). New York: W. H. Freeman, 1995.

WEB SITES

42eXplore: Nuclear Age
www.42explore.com/nuclear.htm
 This Web site covers the history and present-day use of nuclear energy.

The Manhattan Project Heritage Preservation Association, Inc.
www.childrenofthemanhattanproject.org/index.htm
This huge Web site has special sections for students, with information on all aspects of the Manhattan Project.

The Spirit of Hiroshima
http://hiroshima.tomato.nu/English/index_e.html
This Web site from Japan includes many links to learn about the effects of the atomic bomb on the Japanese people and their plea for world peace.

NOTES

1. Pyramid Films, *The Day After Trinity*, produced by Jon Else for KTEH: San Jose, CA, videocassette, 88 minutes. MacArthur Video Library, 1980.
2. Quoted in Richard Rhodes, *The Making of the Atomic Bomb*. New York: Simon and Schuster, 1986, p. 676.
3. Quoted in Peter Michelmore, *The Swift Years: The Robert Oppenheimer Story*. New York: Dodd, Mead, 1969, p. 28.
4. Quoted in Nuel Pharr Davis, *Lawrence and Oppenheimer*. New York: Simon and Schuster, 1968, p. 254.
5. Quoted in Stephane Groueff, *Manhattan Project: The Untold Story of the Making of the Atomic Bomb*. New York: Bantam, 1968, p. 45.
6. Quoted in Rhodes, *The Making of the Atomic Bomb*, pp. 448–449.
7. Quoted in Davis, *Lawrence and Oppenheimer*, p. 177.
8. Quoted in Alice Kimball Smith and Charles Weiner, eds., *Robert Oppenheimer Letters and Recollections*. Cambridge, MA: Harvard University Press, 1980, pp. 262–263.
9. Quoted in Rhodes, *The Making of the Atomic Bomb*, p. 570.
10. Quoted in Lansing Lamont, *Day of Trinity*. New York: Signet, 1966, p. 80.
11. Quoted in Lamont, *Day of Trinity*, p. 132.
12. Quoted in Lamont, *Day of Trinity*, p. 181.
13. Quoted in Lamont, *Day of Trinity*, p. 186.
14. Quoted in Michelmore, *The Swift Years*, p. 113.
15. Quoted in Rhodes, *The Making of the Atomic Bomb*, p. 758.
16. Quoted in Davis, *Lawrence and Oppenheimer*, p. 355.
17. Quoted in Michelmore, *The Swift Years*, p. 254.
18. Quoted in Philip Stern, *The Oppenheimer Case*. New York: Harper and Row, 1969, p. 502.
19. Quoted in Stern, *The Oppenheimer Case*, p. 502.
20. Quoted in Rhodes, *The Making of the Atomic Bomb*, Part One title page.

INDEX